Teaching Kids The Holy Quran – Surah 18: The Cave

As translated and illustrated by:

MEZBA UDDIN MAHTAB

ISBN: 1492331023
ISBN-13: 978-1492331025

DEDICATION

To my mother, Rizwana, for always encouraging me to read, learn and strive for excellence.

To my father, Abujafar, for teaching me to read the *Holy Quran* and love Islam.

To my siblings, Samiha and Munir, for being my constant cheerleaders and my inspiration.

To my wife, Sana, for giving me unconditional encouragement, love and patience.

And finally, for my son Yusuf, who will inherit the world and make it a much better place, God willing.

All Praise is due to Allah, we praise Him and we seek help from Him. We ask forgiveness from Him. We repent to Him and we seek refuge in Him from our own evils and our own bad deeds. Anyone who is guided by Allah is indeed guided, and anyone who has been left astray will find no one to guide him. I bear witness that there is no god but Allah, the Only One without any partner, and I bear witness that Muhammad (peace be upon him) is His servant and His final messenger.

This book is a translation and illustration of the *Holy Quran*, Chapter 18. If there are any mistakes, the fault is entirely mine, and I seek Allah's forgiveness. If you find my work beneficial, all good things come from Allah.

Printed by CreateSpace.

Cover page design (front) by Munir Uddin Mahtab, Sana Ahmed and Samiha Mahtab.
Cover page design (back) by Munir Uddin Mahtab and Sana Ahmed.
Interior artwork by Mezba Uddin Mahtab.

ABOUT THE "READ WITH MEANING" PROJECT

Read With Meaning is a one man labour of love, started in 2010. It contains over 1000 illustrations of verses from the *Holy Quran*, constructed and photographed entirely by Mezba. It is the largest, most comprehensive blog for pictures depicting stories from the *Holy Quran*, translated and with exegesis, maintained entirely by Mezba. The website was awarded the prestigious Brass Crescent Award in 2011, winning in the Best New Blog category. Mezba's work was featured in Muslimfest 2012 and 2013, a world renowned two-day exhibition in the Greater Toronto Area that celebrates the best in Muslim arts and entertainment. The site has also been highlighted in various blogs and publications such as Albawaba, AMuslima, Godbricks, Iqra.ca, Khaleejesque, MuslimMatters, Philosufi, The Purple Journal and Muslimness.

Follow 'Read With Meaning' on Facebook: https://www.facebook.com/readwithmeaning
Twitter: @quran4kids
Blog: http://readwithmeaning.wordpress.com/

WHY PORTRAY THE *HOLY QURAN* WITH TOYS?

I did this primarily for two groups.

First, Muslims who usually just read the Noble Book in Arabic without understanding a word of what they are reciting by rote. Kids are taught from an early age that it is more important to read the *Holy Quran* than to understand it. They seem to have taken the first revealed word – "Read" – a little too literally! I hope my work – in presenting the *Holy Quran* in a visual medium – will make kids more interested in finding out the meaning of the words behind their prayers.

Second, for people who may not read the *Holy Quran* at all, such as non-Muslims. Many have a negative impression of Muslims in general, and I hope this book, with the words of God visually represented, helps in them seeing what we hold holy in a better light.

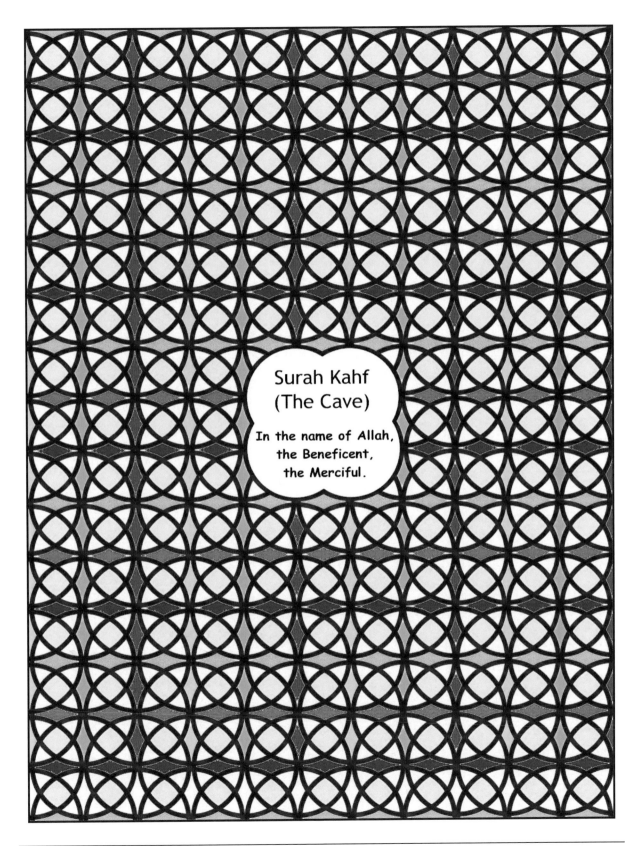

Surah Kahf
(The Cave)

In the name of Allah,
the Beneficent,
the Merciful.

The desert sun beat down mercilessly on two men who were on their way to the town of Yathrib (later to be known to the world as Madinah). The two men were Uqbah and Nadr, and they were travelling from Makkah.

Uqbah, is it not my turn to ride the camel? You have been riding ever since we left Makkah!

The Jews of that time lived in fortresses in and around Yathrib. There were three main Jewish tribes in the city - the Banu Qaynuqa, the Banu Nadir and the Banu Qurayzah.

So he told them, again, "Come back tomorrow. I will tell you the answers then!"

For fifteen days there was no revelation from Allah. The people of Makkah began to taunt the Prophet Muhammad (peace be upon him) and his followers.

Finally, after fifteen long days, Angel Jibrail (Gabriel) appeared with a new revelation - Surah Kahf (The Cave).

001. Praise be to Allah who has revealed the Book unto His slave, and has not placed in it any crookedness.

The Holy Quran remains as pure and free from errors today, as it was when it was revealed over 1400 years ago.

Compare any copy of the Quran today with an ancient one; you will find the words and letters are the same. Allah has protected His Word from corruption.

002. (He has made it) straight, to give warning (to the godless) of stern punishment from Him, and to give good news to the believers who do Righteous Deeds that they shall have a goodly reward.

This world can be a prison for the true Believer, as we have to conduct ourselves with piety in accordance with God's laws and decency. But our true reward is in the Hereafter.

003. Wherein they will
abide for ever.

004. And warn those who say,
"Allah has begotten a son".

005. They have no knowledge of it, nor had their fathers ...

(005) ... *a grievous word it is that comes out of their mouths. They speak nothing but a lie.*

006. Yet it may be, that you would torment yourself to death, sorrowing after them, if they do not believe in this statement.

007. Lo! We have placed all that is on the Earth as an ornament thereof that we may try them (as to) which of them is best in works.

008. And lo! We shall make all that is on it a barren mound.

Question ONE: tell us about the young men who had left their city in the distant past and what had happened to them.

009. Or, do you think that the People of the Cave and the Inscription* were of Our wonderful signs?

*Seven Sleepers of Ephesus

010. When the young men sought refuge in the Cave, they said, "Our Lord! Give us mercy from You, and shape for us a right course in our plight."

011. Then We sealed up their hearing in the Cave for a number of years.

012. Then We roused them, in order to test which of the two parties was best at calculating the time they tarried!

Can you estimate how much time has elapsed while we were asleep?

013. We narrate unto you their story with truth. Lo! They were young men who believed in their Lord, and We increased them in guidance.

014. And We made firm their hearts when they stood forth and said,"Our Lord is the Lord of the heavens and of the earth. Never shall we call upon any god other than Him, for then we would indeed have uttered an enormity!"

015. These, our people, have taken gods besides Him. Why do they not produce any clear authority in their support? And who does greater wrong than he who invents a lie concerning Allah?

016. And when you forsake them and
what they worship save Allah, then
seek refuge in the Cave, your Lord
will spread for you of His mercy and
will prepare for you a profitable course
in your plight.

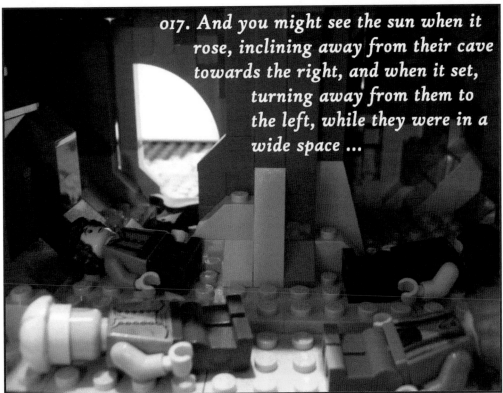

017. And you might see the sun when it
rose, inclining away from their cave
towards the right, and when it set,
turning away from them to
the left, while they were in a
wide space ...

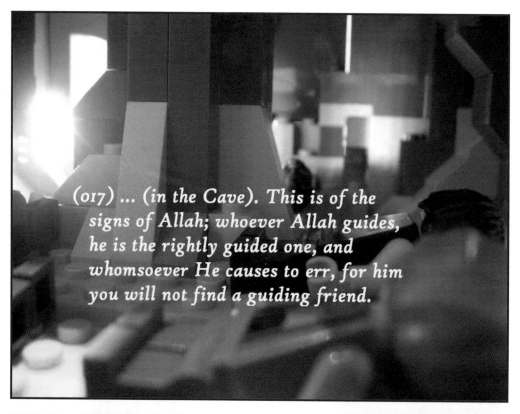

(017) ... (in the Cave). This is of the signs of Allah; whoever Allah guides, he is the rightly guided one, and whomsoever He causes to err, for him you will not find a guiding friend.

018. And you might think them awake while they were asleep and We turned them about to the right and to the left ...

(018) ... while their dog (lay) outstretching its paws at the threshold ...

(018) ... *if you looked at them you would certainly turn back from them in flight, and you would certainly be filled with awe because of them.*

Meanwhile, as the People of the Cave slept, time went on and decades flew by. Over 300 years later, the area was now ruled by a righteous king whose subjects worshipped only Allah alone.

The pious king became sad. He prayed to Allah for a miracle to convince his subjects about the truth of a life after death, and the Day of Judgement, and to keep them on the straight path.

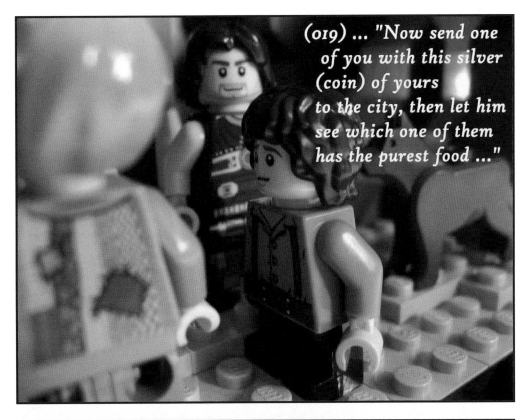

His companions had instructed him to only buy the purest* food.

* Some scholars today state that even in dire circumstances these
  young men were conscious of the Halal and Haram in food.

021. Thus did We make their case known to the people, that they might know that the promise of Allah is true, and that there can be no doubt about the Hour of Judgement ...

(021) ... When (the people of the city) disputed of their case among themselves, they said, "Build over them a building (in honour); their Lord knows best concerning them."

(022) .. say they were seven, the dog being the eighth.

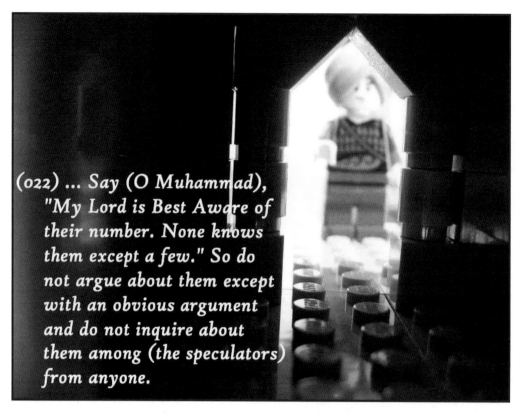

(022) ... Say (O Muhammad), "My Lord is Best Aware of their number. None knows them except a few." So do not argue about them except with an obvious argument and do not inquire about them among (the speculators) from anyone.

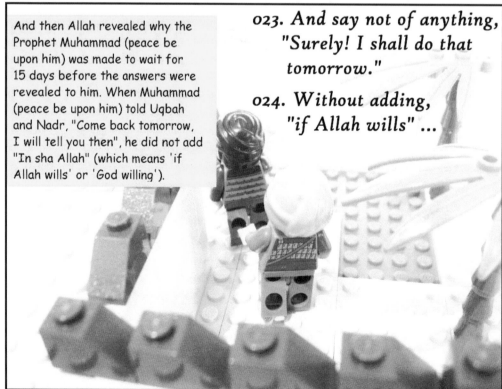

And then Allah revealed why the Prophet Muhammad (peace be upon him) was made to wait for 15 days before the answers were revealed to him. When Muhammad (peace be upon him) told Uqbah and Nadr, "Come back tomorrow, I will tell you then", he did not add "In sha Allah" (which means 'if Allah wills' or 'God willing').

023. And say not of anything, "Surely! I shall do that tomorrow."

024. Without adding, "if Allah wills" ...

This is why we say "In sha Allah" (which translates to 'if Allah wills' or 'God willing') when talking about a future course of action. This is because we do not know if we will live to see this future, and even if we do, whether we will be able to complete the action. No matter how carefully we plan the future and how likely that plan may seem to materialize, the ultimate truth of the matter is that eventually it will materialize only if Allah wills.

I am walking towards the mall. I will be reaching there in about 10 minutes In sha Allah!

(024) ... and remember your Lord when you forget and say, "Maybe my Lord will guide me unto a nearer way of truth than this."

The same was also true regarding the revelations which the Prophet Muhammad (peace be upon him) received from Allah. The Prophet Muhammad (peace be upon him) could not control the revelations - only when Allah willed would the verses of Quran be sent down.

I have to respond to a robbery at the mall. In sha Allah, no one will be hurt, and In sha Allah, I will arrest the criminals.

025. And they remained in their cave for three hundred years and (some) add (another) nine*.

* 300 solar years = 309 lunar years

026. Say, "Allah knows best how long they remained; to Him are (known) the unseen things of the heavens and of the earth; how clear His sight and how clear His hearing! There is none to be a guardian for them besides Him, and He does not make anyone His associate in His command."

027. *And recite what has been revealed to you of the Book of your Lord. There is none who can change His words, and you shall not find any refuge besides Him.*

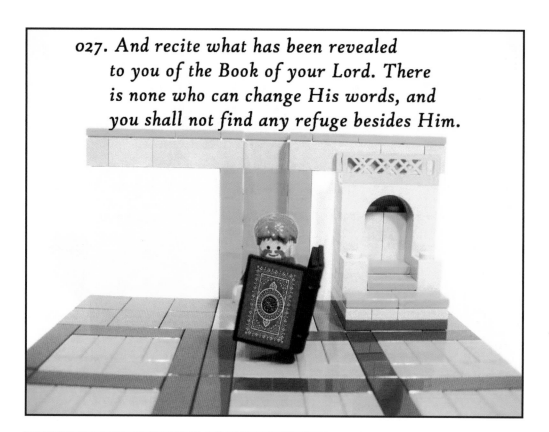

Amongst the earliest disciples of the Prophet Muhammad (peace be upon him) were some (current and former) slaves such as Bilal ibn Rabah and Khabbab ibn al-Aratt. They were poor, and not from the nobility of the Quraish. Someone suggested to Muhammad (peace be upon him) that he should hold a separate gathering for the chiefs of the Quraish where these Companions would not be present.

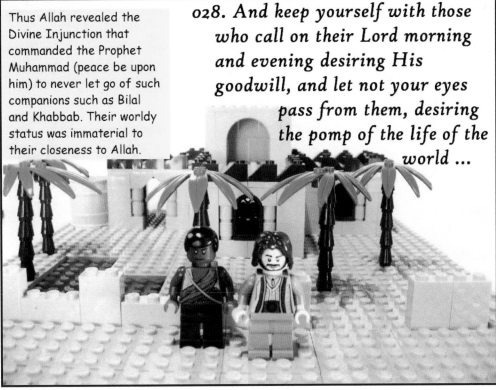

Thus Allah revealed the Divine Injunction that commanded the Prophet Muhammad (peace be upon him) to never let go of such companions such as Bilal and Khabbab. Their worldy status was immaterial to their closeness to Allah.

028. And keep yourself with those who call on their Lord morning and evening desiring His goodwill, and let not your eyes pass from them, desiring the pomp of the life of the world ...

(028) ... *and do not follow him whose heart We have made unmindful to Our remembrance, and he follows his low desires and his case is one in which has gone beyond all bounds.*

029. And say, "The truth is from your Lord, so let him who please, believe, and let him who please, disbelieve. For the wrong-doers We have prepared a Fire; the curtains of which shall encompass them about; and if they cry for water, they will be showered with water like molten lead which burns the faces. Evil the drink and ill the resting place!"

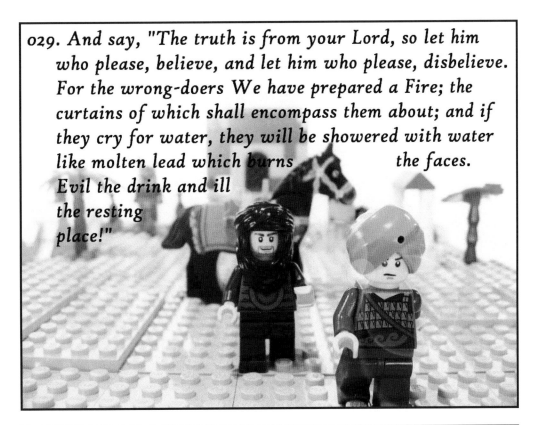

030. As to those who believe and do good deeds ...

(030) ... verily We do not waste the reward of any who does a (single) righteous deed.

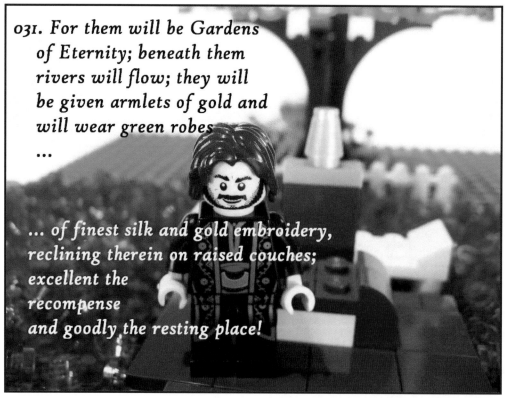

031. For them will be Gardens of Eternity; beneath them rivers will flow; they will be given armlets of gold and will wear green robes ...

... of finest silk and gold embroidery, reclining therein on raised couches; excellent the recompense and goodly the resting place!

032. *And set forth to them a parable of two men ...*

(032) *... for one of them We made two gardens of grape vines, and We surrounded them both with palms, and in the midst of them We made cornfields.*

033. Each of the gardens gave its fruit and withheld nothing thereof ...

(033) ... and We caused a river to flow therein.

034. (Abundant) was the produce this man had ...

(034) ... He said to his companion, in the course of a mutual argument ...

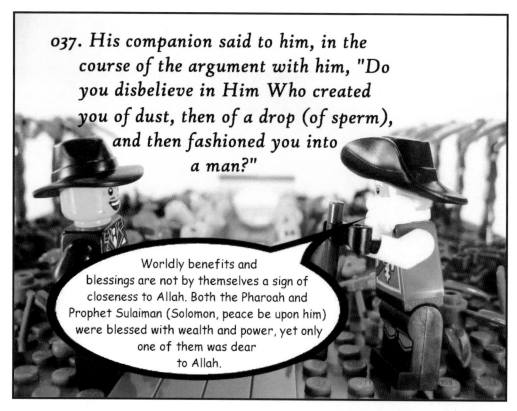

040. "... then maybe my Lord will give me what is better than your garden, and send on yours a calamity from the heavens so that it shall become a smooth, dusty, barren land!"

041. "Or the water of the garden will run off underground so that you will never be able to find it."

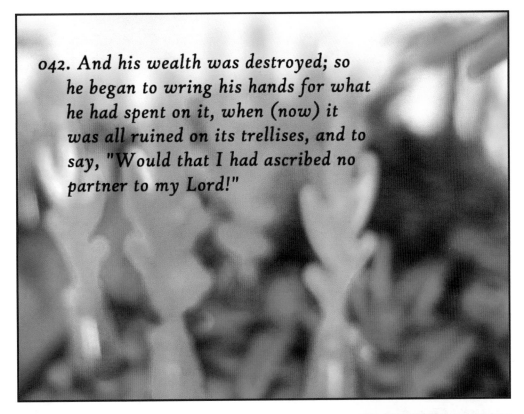

042. And his wealth was destroyed; so he began to wring his hands for what he had spent on it, when (now) it was all ruined on its trellises, and to say, "Would that I had ascribed no partner to my Lord!"

043. And there was for him no company to aid him other than Allah, nor could he save himself.

044. There, the (only) protection comes from Allah, the True. He is the Best to reward, and the Best to give success.

045. Set forth to them the similitude of the life of this world - it is like the rain which We send down from the sky, and the earth's vegetation absorbs it ...

(045) ... but soon it becomes dry stubble, which the winds do scatter. It is (only) Allah who prevails over all things.

047. One Day We shall remove the mountains, and you will see the earth as a level stretch ...

(047) ... and We shall gather them
together and not leave behind
from them anyone.
048. And they shall be brought before
your Lord, standing in ranks (with
announcement), "Now verily have
you come unto Us as We created you
first. But you thought that We had
set no tryst for you!"

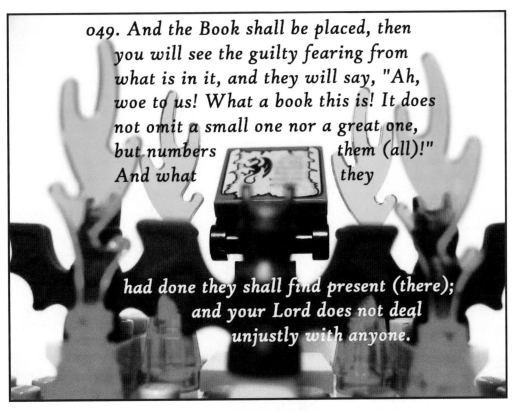

049. And the Book shall be placed, then you will see the guilty fearing from what is in it, and they will say, "Ah, woe to us! What a book this is! It does not omit a small one nor a great one, but numbers them (all)!" And what they had done they shall find present (there); and your Lord does not deal unjustly with anyone.

050. Behold! We said to the angels, "Bow down to Adam". They bowed down except Iblis ...

I am created from fire, and Adam is created from clay. Why should I bow down to him?

051. I did not make them witness the creation of the heavens and the earth, nor their own creation. And I am not the one to take those who mislead as helpers!

052. And the Day He will say, "Call on those whom you thought to be My partners", and they will call on them, but they will not hear their prayer, and We shall set a gulf of doom between them.

053. And the sinners will see the Fire, so they will know that they are to fall into it and they will find no way to bypass it.

054. We have explained in detail in this Quran, for the benefit of mankind, every kind of similitude, but man is, of all things, most contentious.

How can a book revealed centuries ago be considered relavant for modern times? It's just tales of the Old. If God is so Powerful, why does he not send down His Wrath on us, for our 'sins'?

055. And nothing prevents men from believing when the guidance comes to them, and from asking forgiveness of their Lord, but that (they ask that) the ways of the ancients be repeated with them, or the Wrath be brought to them face to face.

056. And We do not send the Messengers but as bearers of good tidings and warnings, and those who disbelieve raise disputes with the false (arguments) so that they may nullify the truth.

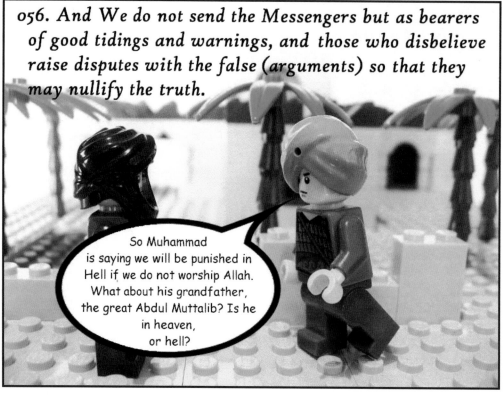

(057) ... Surely We have placed veils over their hearts lest they should understand it and a heaviness in their ears; and if you call them to the guidance, they will not ever follow the right course in that case.

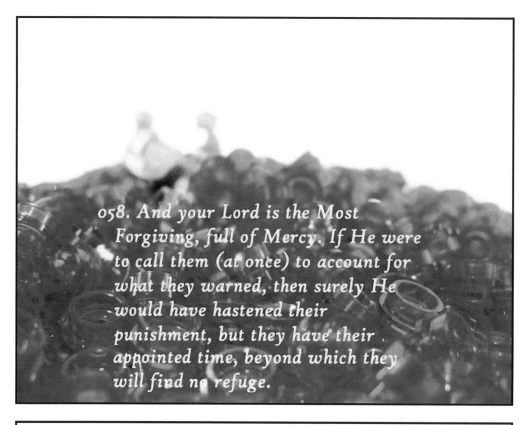

058. And your Lord is the Most Forgiving, full of Mercy. If He were to call them (at once) to account for what they warned, then surely He would have hastened their punishment, but they have their appointed time, beyond which they will find no refuge.

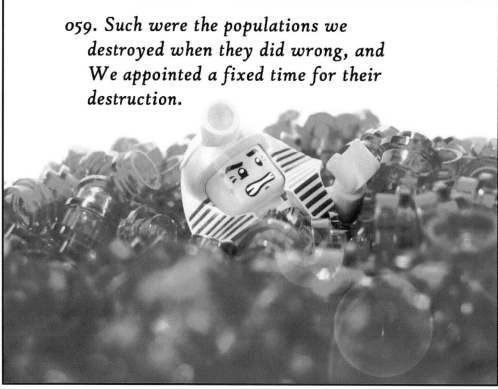

059. Such were the populations we destroyed when they did wrong, and We appointed a fixed time for their destruction.

The next section of Surah Kahf talks about the meeting between Prophet Musa (Moses, peace be upon him) and Al Khidr (the Green One), a righteous servant of Allah.

It so happened that once Musa (peace be upon him) was addressing the Children of Israel when someone asked him a question.

Sometime, during the life of Prophet Musa (Moses, peace be upon him) ...

Who is the most knowledgeable person in the world, amongst all of creation?

061. But when they had reached the junction (of the two seas), they forgot (about) their fish ...

(061) ... which took its course though the sea, as in a tunnel.

062. And when they had gone further, Musa said to his servant, "Bring us our breakfast. Verily we have found fatigue in this our journey."

063. He replied, "Did you see when we took refuge on the rock then I forgot the fish, and nothing made me forget to speak of it but Satan, and it took its way into the sea; what a wonder!"

064. Musa said, "This is that which we have been seeking". So they retraced their steps again.

065. So they found one of Our slaves, on whom We had bestowed Mercy from Ourselves and whom We had taught knowledge from Our Own Presence.

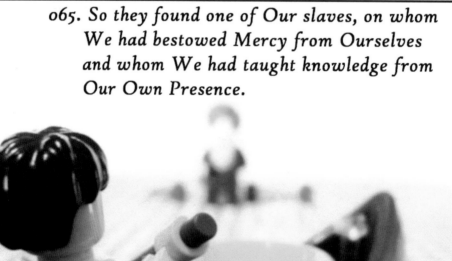

066. Musa said to him, "May I follow you on condition that you teach me something of the (Higher) Truth which you have been taught?

067. He (the other) replied, "Surely you cannot have patience with me!"

068. "And how can you have patience in that of which you have not got a comprehensive knowledge?"

069. Musa said, "You will find me, if Allah wills, (truly) patient, and I shall not disobey you in any matter."

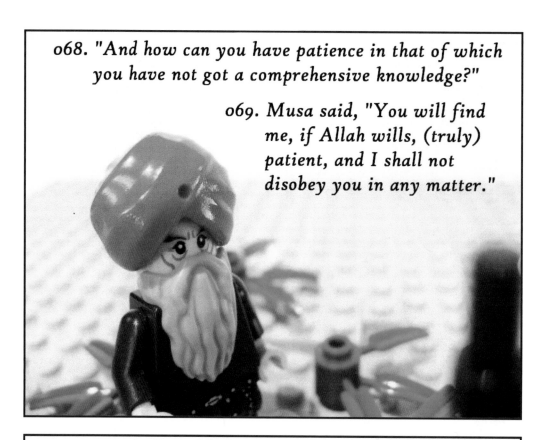

070. He said (to Musa), "If you would follow me, then do not question me about any thing until I myself speak to you about it."

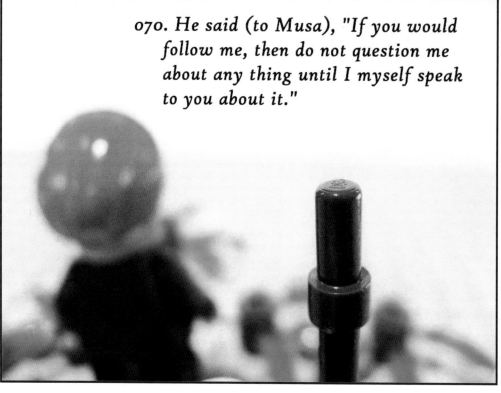

(071) ... until, when they were in a boat, he (Al Khidr) made a hole in it. Musa said, "Have you scuttled it in order to drown those in it? Truly a strange thing have you done!"

072. He said, "Did I not say that you will not be able to have patience with me?"

073. Musa replied, "Rebuke me not for forgetting, and be not hard upon me for my fault."

While they were on the boat, a bird flew down and sat on the edge of the boat, and dipped its beak once or twice into the sea.

074. So they went on ...

(074) ... Musa said, "Have you slain an innocent person who had slain none? Certainly you have done an evil thing!"

075. He said, "Did I not tell you that you will not be able to bear with me?"

076. Musa said, "If I ask you about anything after this, keep me not in your company. Indeed you shall have (then) found an excuse in my case."

077. So they went on until when they came to the people of a (certain) town.

(077) ... They asked them for food, but they refused to entertain them as guests.

(077) ... Then they found in it a wall which was on the point of falling ...

(077) ... and he (Al Khidr) repaired it.

(077) ... Musa said, "If you had wished, you could have taken payment for it."

078. He (Al Khidr) said, "This is the parting between me and you. Now I will tell you the interpretation of that with which you could not have patience."

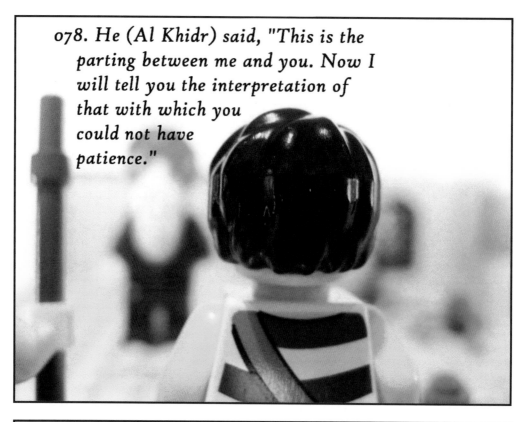

079. "As for the (damaged) boat, it belonged to poor people working on the river but I wished to render it unserviceable, for there was after them a certain king who seized on every boat by force."

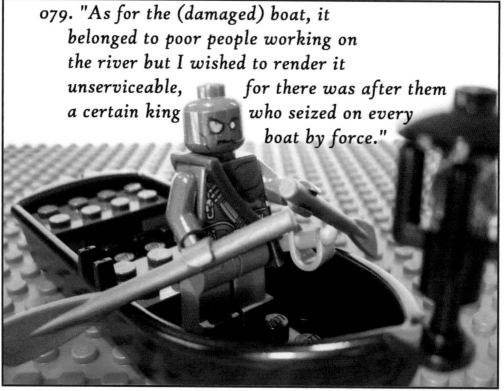

080. "And as for the (slain) young man,
his parents were people of
Faith ..."

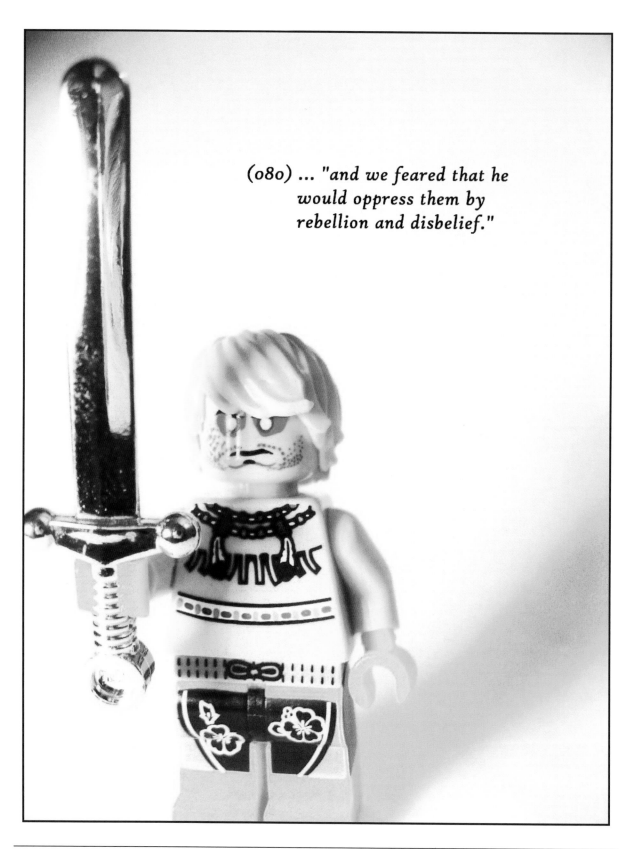

(080) ... "and we feared that he would oppress them by rebellion and disbelief."

081. "So we desired that their Lord might give them in his place one better than him in purity and closer in affection."

082. "As for the wall, it belonged to two youths, orphans, in the town ..."

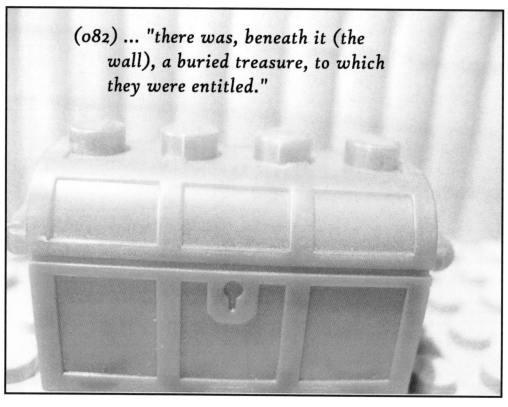

(082) ... "there was, beneath it (the wall), a buried treasure, to which they were entitled."

(082) ... "Their father had been a righteous man."

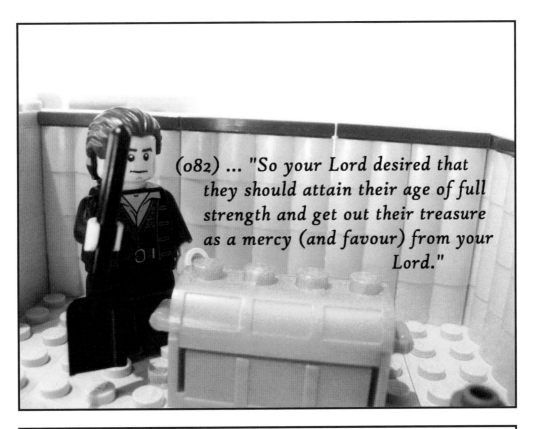

083. They ask you about Zul Qarnayn. Say, "I will recite to you an account of him."

084. Lo! We made him strong in the land and granted him the means of access to every thing.

085. And he followed a road.

086. Until, when he reached the place where the sun set, he found it setting in a muddy spring ...

Muslim scholars have differed over where in the West this place is where Zul Qarnayn observed the sunset. Some say it was the Maghreb (Northwest Africa) and the Atlantic coast, others say it was the eastern coast of the Caspian Sea. Allah knows best.

Glory be to Allah! What a beautiful sunset by the coast!

(086) ... and found by it a people.

Do not associate anyone with Allah in worship. Always speak the truth and be faithful to your trust. The strong amongst you should never exploit the weak. Be kind to your relations. Establish prayer and give charity.

088. And as for him who believes, and does good, he shall have a goodly reward, and We will speak to him an easy word of Our command.

089. Then he followed (another) road.

090. *Until, when he reached the land of the rising of the sun, he found it rising on a people for whom We had provided no shelter from it.*

Where is this land of the "rising of the sun"? Scholars are not sure. Some have said Zul Qarnayn reached the Far East, others have said this was an African desert (Sahara) whose inhabitants lived in tunnels at noon to escape the hot sun. Again, Allah knows best.

091. *(He left them) as they were. We completely understood what was before him.*

092. *Then he followed (another) course.*

093. Till, when he came (to a place) between the two mountains ...

(093) ... he found, beneath them, a people who could hardly understand a word (of his speech).

094. They said, "O Zul Qarnayn! The (People of) Yajuj and Majuj (Gog and Magog) do great mischief on earth ..."

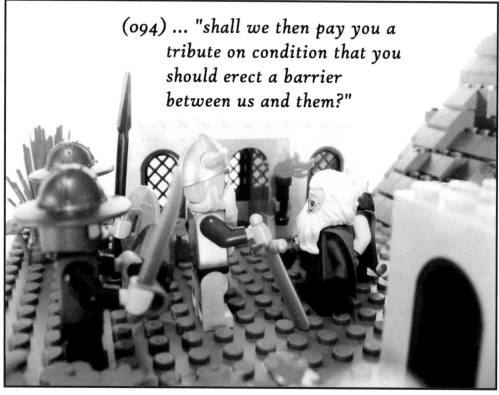

(094) ... "shall we then pay you a tribute on condition that you should erect a barrier between us and them?"

095. He said, "(The power) in which my Lord has established me is better (than tribute). Do but help me ..."

(095) ... "with strength (of the labour of men); I will make a fortified barrier between you and them."

096. (He said) "Bring me blocks of iron."

(096) ... At length, when he had filled up the space between the two steep mountain sides ...

(096) ... He said, "Blow (with your bellows)!" Then, when he had made it (red) as fire ...

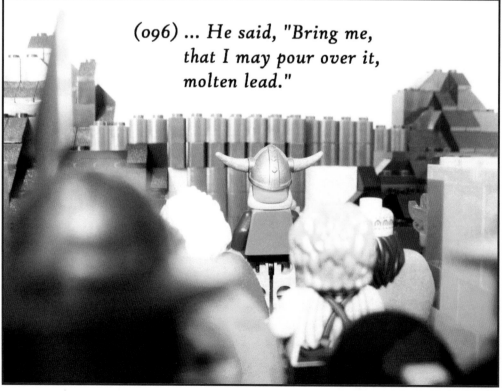

(096) ... He said, "Bring me, that I may pour over it, molten lead."

097. *Thus they were made powerless to scale it or to dig through it.*

According to a narration on whose isnad (chain of transmission) there is some ikhtilaf (scholarly disagreement), the people of Yajuj and Majuj (Gog and Magog) keep digging through the wall of Zul Qarnayn everyday.

By digging all day, at last they will reach a stage where a sliver of light from the other side becomes visible to them. The people of Yajuj and Majuj (Gog and Magog) have almost succeeded in digging a hole through, and have reached the farthest part of Zul Qarnayn's iron wall.

They will then tell each other, "We will finish digging through the rest of the wall tomorrow." Crucially, they do not add "if Allah wills". They drop their tools and plan to return the following morning to complete the job.

However, when they return the following morning, they will find that Allah has restored the wall to as it was before. All their efforts have been for vain, and they will have to start digging all over again. This cycle of their effort to dig and demolish, and that of mending and fortifying from Allah's side will continue until such time up to which Allah intends to hold back the Yajuj and Majuj.

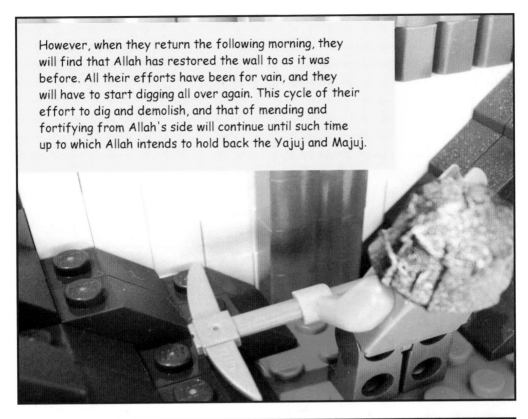

It is from Allah's mercy that the people of Yajuj and Majuj do not think of working continuously via shifts, or of scaling or climbing the wall, or of adding the words "if Allah wills" until the end of time when Allah wills to release them. They will then add the crucial words, "If Allah wills, we shall go across it tomorrow", and the following day, the wall will not have been restored. They would then break through and be let loose upon the world. Upon completing the construction of the wall, Zul Qarnayn warned humanity of this.

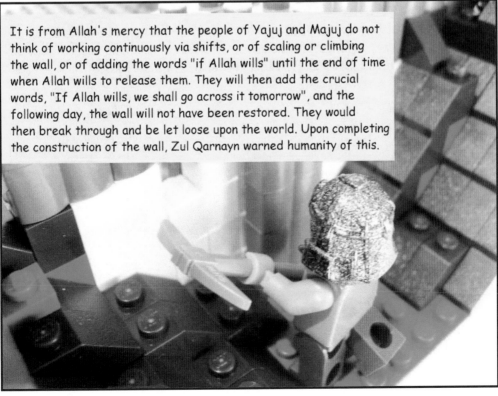

098. He said, "This is a mercy from my Lord, but when the promise of my Lord comes to pass ..."

(098) ... "He will make it into dust; and the promise of my Lord is true."

Along with the Dajjal (the Anti-Christ), the coming of Prophet Isa (Jesus, peace be upon him), and the righteous Imam Mahdi, the release of the people of Yajuj and Majuj (Gog and Magog) will be one of the major signs of the Last Hour. Allah will save the believers from the Yajuj and Majuj through a prayer of Prophet Isa (peace be upon him).

099. And on that day We shall let some of them surge against others, and the Trumpet will be blown. Then We shall gather them together in one gathering.

100. On that day We shall present Hell to the Unbelievers, exposed to view.

101. Those whose eyes were under a veil from My Reminder, and they could not even (bear to) listen.

104. "Those whose efforts have been wasted in this life, while they thought that they were acquiring good by their works."

105. They are those who deny the Signs
     of their Lord and the fact of their
     having to meet Him (in the Hereafter).
     Vain will be their works, nor shall
     We, on the Day of Judgment, give
     them any weight.

106. That is their reward, Hell, because they rejected Faith, and took My Signs and My Messengers by way of jest.

107. Lo! Those who believe and do good
   works, their place of entertainment
   shall be the Gardens of Paradise.

108. Wherein they will abide, with no
   desire to be removed from thence.

109. Say, "If the sea were ink for
   (writing) the Words of my Lord, the
   sea would surely be exhausted before
   the Words of my Lord were exhausted,
   even if We added another sea like it,
   for its aid."

110. *Say, "I am only a man like you. It has been revealed to me that your God is only One God. So whoever hopes for the meeting with his Lord, let him do righteous deeds and not associate anyone in the worship of his Lord."*

ABOUT THE AUTHOR

Mezba Uddin Mahtab is a freelance writer, eBook author, and former Editor-in-Chief of *The Underground*, a campus newspaper at the University of Toronto. Mezba also maintains a personal blog at *A Bengali in TO*. His opinion on issues related to immigration and diversity has been sought for and quoted in interviews in The Toronto Star (Canada), as well as the National (UAE). From 2005 to 2008, Mezba blogged prolifically, attracting coverage from multiple sources such as the Washington Post (USA), the Daily Star (Bangladesh) and the Toronto Star (Canada). Topics often included diverse and controversial issues such as the place of women in the mosque, the role of Islam in the government, the Katrina disaster, Canadian politics and reflections of a single Muslim guy growing up in a Western society.

A Bangladeshi by birth, Mezba was brought up in Abu Dhabi, UAE, where he was taught the *Holy Quran* by Sheikh Siddiqullah, a renowned Bangladeshi *mufassir* (an author of an exegesis of the *Holy Quran*) who was also employed by the UAE royal family as an Islamic teacher. Mezba completed his undergraduate studies in Computer Science at the University of Toronto and later went on to complete an MBA from the Rotman School of Business. He currently works in the IT industry as a software consultant and lives in Toronto, Canada, with his wife Sana and his son Yusuf.

Twitter: @a_bong
Blog: http://mezba.blogspot.ca

Made in the USA
Lexington, KY
16 May 2014